Made in United States
North Haven, CT
10 March 2023

33884766R00035